GUITAR SCALES MADE SIMPLE

CHRIS D

Copywrite@2022

TABLE OF CONTENTS

CHAPTER 1 3
  INTRODUCTION 3
CHAPTER 2 8
  THE MAJOR SCALE 8
CHAPTER 3 11
  THE MINOR SCALE 11
CHAPTER 4 16
  THE MELODIC MINOR SCALE 16
CHAPTER 5 25
  THE BLUES SCALE 25
CHAPTER 6 30
  STEP BY STEP INSTRUCTIONS TO REHEARSE SCALES 30

CHAPTER 1

INTRODUCTION

Scales create a ton of turmoil for guitar students, so before we take a gander at the different scale designs it's significant we make a couple of things understood.

WHAT MAKES LEARNING GUITER SCALES IMPORTANT

Scales are the underpinning of all lead guitar work and make it simple for you to put out wonderful single-note tunes.

At the point when individuals begin to learn guitar scales they accidentally cross a 'scaffold' and begin understanding music hypothesis. This makes you a fundamentally better guitarist since you start to really comprehend the instrument.

when would it be advisable for me to learn guitar scales?

It's never too soon or past time to learn guitar scales. They are advantageous to know at any phase of your guitar venture.

I incline toward complete novices to zero in on harmonies, however I could never deter any individual who needed to gain guitar scales from doing as such. This is valuable stuff.

.

Alright, so what is a scale?

A scale is a progression of steps between two fixed melodic places.

These two fixed focuses are consistently a similar note, yet in various octaves. We refer to these focuses as "root notes".

How we get from the lower root note to the higher root note is known as 'a scale'.

Pay attention to this model. (I utilize two G notes in this model, yet it very well may be any note. The guideline stays valid for ALL notes.)

Guitar scales are essentially 'examples of notes'

In all out there are 12 notes that COULD be played between the lower root note and higher root note. (This is a full octave.)

- Consider it a stepping stool with 12 'rungs'. The stepping stool addresses the octave.

- The first crosspiece and the twelfth bar are dependably there, consistently in a similar spot, yet the example of rungs in the middle can change.

- The example of the rungs on the stepping stool addresses the different scale designs.

Since there are 12 'rungs' (AKA 'notes') there are bunches of various examples and stages that we can decide to join them in.

I frequently see individuals attempting to learn guitar scales get overpowered by how much examples, yet all at once fortunately it's actual basic.

There are several scale designs that close to 100% of guitarists need to know and we will go through them here.

Would you be able to understand chords and scale diagram?

To get what's approaching next you should have the option to peruse harmony outlines (AKA 'chordboxes').

All of the scale outlines in this guide follow this design:

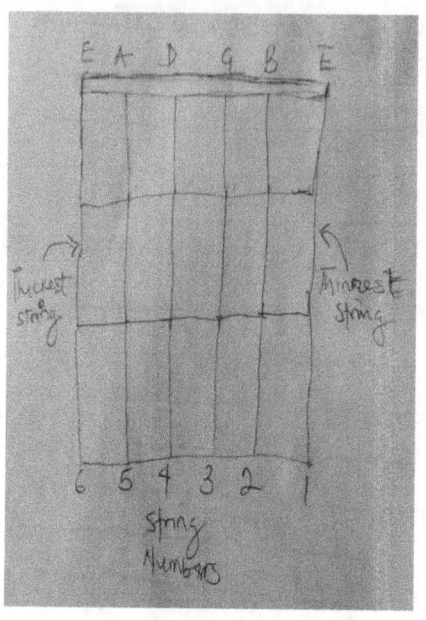

Alright, you buy this article to learn guitar scales so how about we check out our first scale!

CHAPTER 2

THE MAJOR SCALE

It is fundamental to see how the significant scale functions in light of the fact that its example is the measuring stick by which we portray some other melodic sound.

Each harmony and scale is named by how it analyzes to this scale. To learn guitar scales this is the best beginning stage.

This is a splendid and blissful sounding scale. It's inspiring, sweet and hopeful.

Box 1 of the significant scale resembles this (we'll discuss 'boxes' later on):

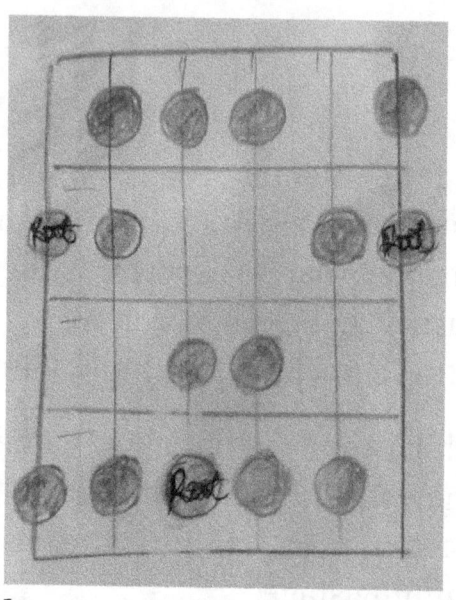

Did you recognize the three root notes here? Good job!.

Scales are moveable in patterns

A pivotal point you should know whether you need to learn guitar scales is that scale designs are MOVEABLE.

What directs the resonance of the scale is the place where you BEGIN playing it.

Assuming you begin playing the above design on the fifth fret (so the root note on the left is on the fifth fret of the sixth string) you will play the **A Major Scale.**

In the event that you play similar example from a beginning position two frets higher (beginning the seventh fret) you will play the **B Major Scale.**

.

A scale's root note is the legend note or the hero note. Use it parcels.

In each scale there is a root note. The root note names the scale.

In the E Major Scale the root note is E.

The root note is the legend note. The note will sound best and give a feeling of goal to the riffs, licks and performances that you play. Finish your expressions on the root note to make what you played sound 'right'.

CHAPTER 3

THE MINOR SCALE

The other scale that you should know whether you need to learn guitar scales is the Minor Scale.

There are three distinct sorts of minor scope:

- The Natural Minor Scale (it is fundamental that you know this scale)

- The Harmonic Minor Scale (this is a cool scale and you should realize this, yet at the same it's not fundamental)

- The Melodic Minor Scale (it's not fundamental that you realize this scale)

At the point when individuals talk about "the minor scope" they are quite often alluding to the Natural

Minor Scale. That is the 'fundamental' rendition of these three minor scopes.

The Minor Scale is a lot cooler than the Major Scale

The Natural Minor Scale gives a contrast to the Major Scale. To learn guitar scales you really want to comprehend the disposition they make. This scale sounds dismal and despairing and the differentiation from the Major Scale is distinct.

Obviously, we want both! (Yin and Yang. Light and dim. Batman and the Joker, and so forth... !)

I think the Natural Minor Scale is a lot cooler than the Major Scale, it sounds really fascinating and reminiscent.

Be that as it may, maybe the best part is that it gives us the establishment for the Minor Pentatonic Scale and Blues Scale which are the best time scales for most of guitarists. (We'll cover both of these scales later on in this aide.)

Obviously, I'm in good company to like the Natural Minor Scale since this scale gives the establishment to practically all rock and blues lead guitar. (Playing a solo in a minor scope over significant harmonies simply sounds magnificent. I've been doing it for a really long time and it gets increasingly more fun as time passes by!)

The Natural Minor Scale resembles this:

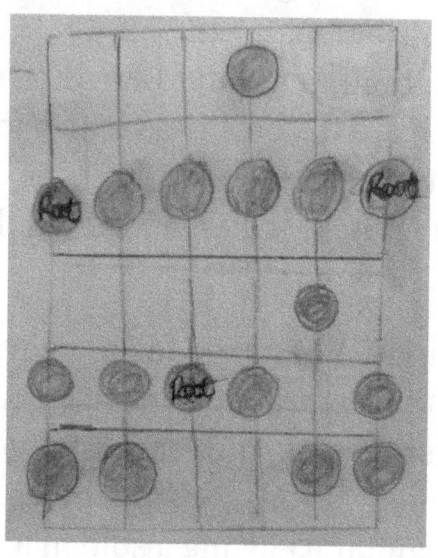

Actually, this scale 'closes' on the root note at the right, yet individuals will more often than not add on the two notes on the extreme right. (These notes are from the beginning of the following octave.) I utilize these notes since they generally sound great. The Harmonic or Melodic Minor Scale

This is just somewhat unique to the Natural Minor Scale. Here we hone the penultimate note to make the draw back to the root note more grounded.

This makes an outlandish sounding 3-venture stretch. Attempt it!

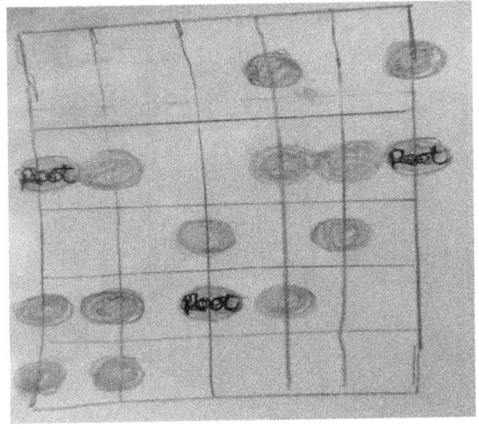

Top tip: When soloing you can mix these two minor scopes together and play a 'half and half' scale like this:

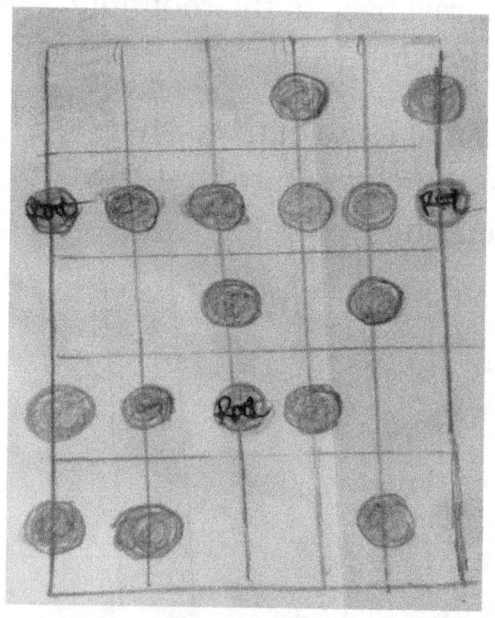

CHAPTER 4

THE MELODIC MINOR SCALE

In more conventional types of music that 3-venture stretch isn't wanted. So we add an additional a note to smooth the rising. This makes the 'melodic minor scope'. (Otherwise known as Jazz Melodic Minor Scale.) It resembles this:

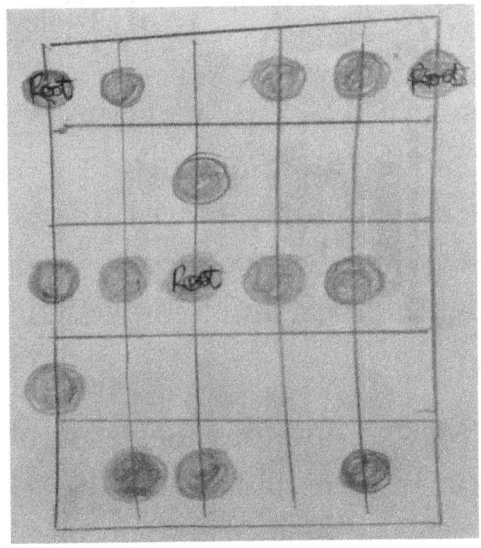

Except if you need to learn jazz this is a beautiful specialty scale. Most guitarists won't have to know it.

MAJOR AND MINOR PENTATONIC SCALES

Up to this point we've covered the two mainstays of music scale hypothesis: the Major Scale and the Minor Scale.

These two scales are major and you should know about them, yet most transitional guitarists play these two scales in a more straightforward and abbreviated structure.

The Major Pentatonic Scale is the Major Scale in abbreviated structure.

So rather than playing the full significant scale design like this:

The Major Scale

We play an easier form, similar to this:

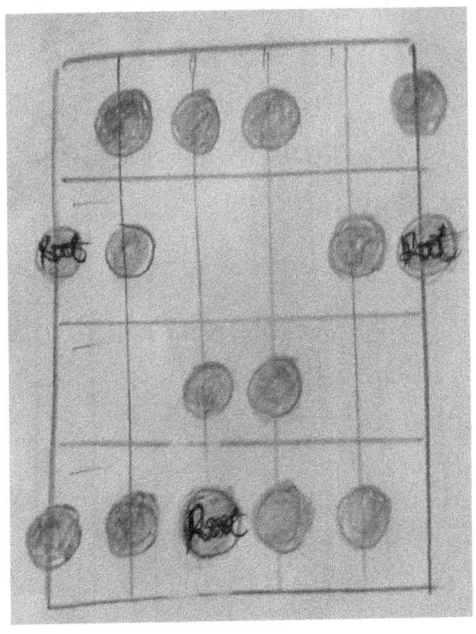

The Major Pentatonic Scale

Would you be able to see that we basically eliminated two notes from every octave? (4 notes altogether.)

I frequently see guitar students wrongly think the Major Scale is an entirely unexpected scale to the Major Pentatonic Scale. No, the Major Pentatonic Scale IS the Major Scale, in a less difficult structure.

Essentially, the Minor Pentatonic Scale is the Minor Scale in compressed structure.

So rather than playing this:

The Natural Minor Scale

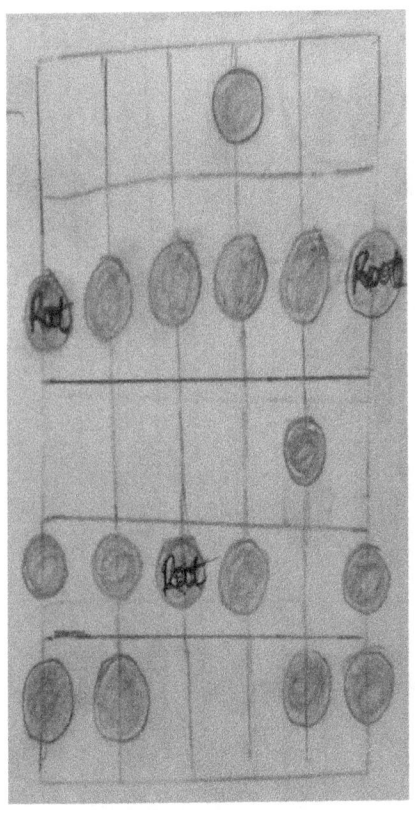

We play this:

The Minor Pentatonic Scale

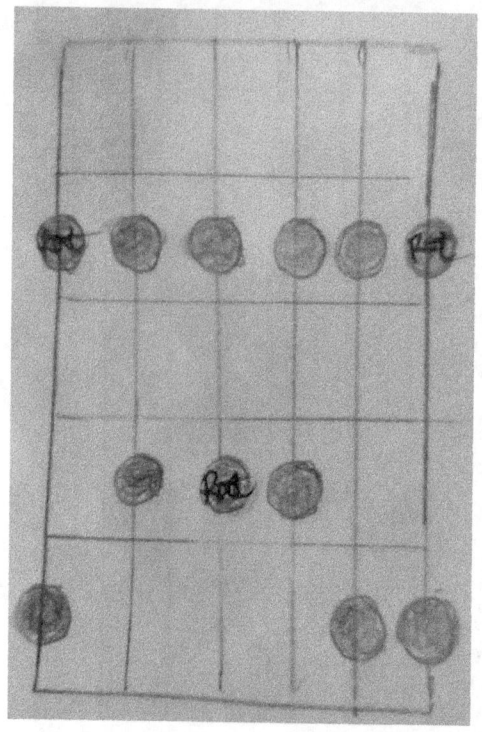

Would you be able to perceive how everything we've done here is eliminate two notes from every octave? (4 notes eliminated altogether.)

So assuming you figure out how to play the Major Scale and the Minor Scale you definitely 'know' how to play their pentatonic renditions. You simply need to get acclimated with forgetting about those two notes in every octave.

Box 1 of the Major Pentatonic Scale resembles this:

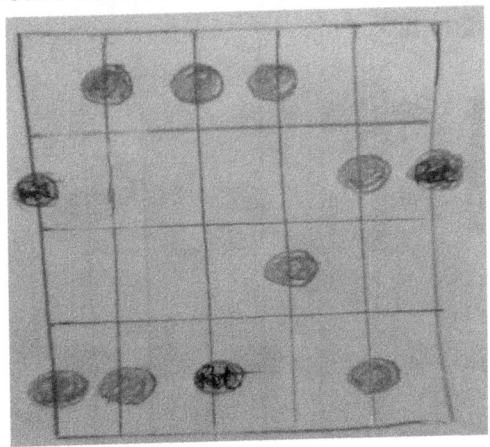

This isn't the least demanding scale to solo with, so by far most of middle guitarists use box 1 of the Minor Pentatonic Scale for most of their lead guitar work.

In the event that you gain just something single from this illustration it ought to be to realize this example:

Minor Pentatonic Scale (Box 1)

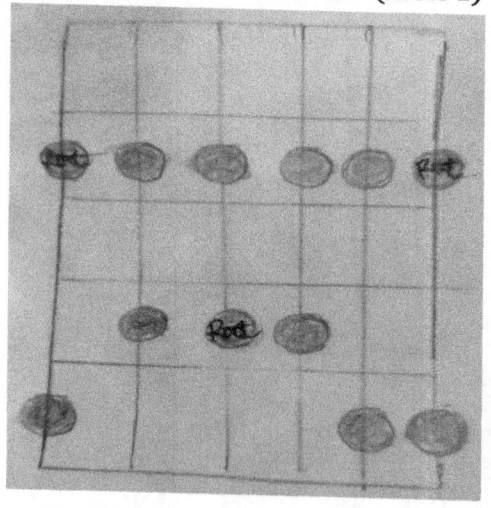

The Minor Pentatonic Scale is the best scale to learn to learn guitar scales to play performances and lead guitar.

In a second we'll take a gander at perhaps the coolest size of every one of, the Blues Scale. Before we do, we should have a speedy talk about 'boxes'. (To learn guitar scales you want to know this.)

An easy note on 'boxes'

The guitar neck is long and the notes cross-over starting with one string then onto the next. It is basically impossible that we can retain every one of the examples in one go.

- To make life simpler for ourselves we partition all scales on the neck into 5 portions to make things more sensible.

- You can play each scale in each section. We call these portions 'boxes'.

- This is overpowering! So we do what we generally do. We improve.

- We break this long example into 5 more limited examples. These 5 more modest examples are called 'boxes'.

- According to a music hypothesis perspective, the notes in each of the 5 in a E minor Pentatonic scale boxes follows a similar melodic example. They are a similar scale.

- However, when these notes are spread out across the guitar fretboard the fives boxes appear to be extremely unique from each other.

- They all share a similar melodic 'DNA', however their appearance is changed.

That implies we need to get familiar with various examples to play similar scale in various situations on the guitar neck.

Try not to stress over learning boxes 2, 3, 4 and 5 at the present time. Simply center around box 1 for each scale.

Ace box 1 of each scale prior to endeavoring others

In this article, to keep things basic, we've quite recently involved box 1 for each scale. This is the means by which you should move toward this as well.

This is by a wide margin the most effective way to learn guitar scales. Simply learn box 1's for the time being, however realize that there are 4 additional cases for each scale. You can move onto these later on! ⍰

Alright how about we check out my cherished size of every one of, the Blues Scale. To this end we learn guitar scales!

CHAPTER 5

THE BLUES SCALE

The Blues Scale is an exceptionally direct relation of the Minor Pentatonic Scale. It sounds marvelous in most stone, independent, nation and blues situations.

It resembles this:

The Blues Scale

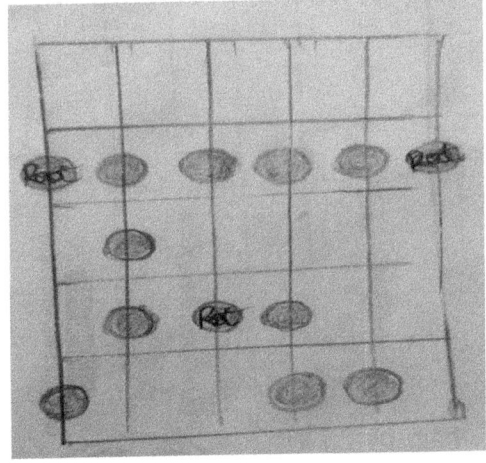

Perhaps the coolest thing about the Blues Scale is that you can regularly play it over both major and minor keys.

It won't work over each harmony movement, however it takes care of business over parcels. It's an adaptable scale.

Assuming you're attempting to learn guitar scales this is a gigantic lift, since it makes everything simpler.

.

Keys

To learn guitar scales since you expect to play lead guitar you really want to know this:

The least demanding method for playing lead guitar that will sound "great" is to play notes from a scale that matches the melody's critical.

This is so significant I'm going to re-type it!!

The least demanding method for playing lead guitar that will sound "great" is to play notes from a scale that matches the melody's critical.

So assuming that the key of a tune is C Major, you will sound wonderful in the event that you play a riff or solo with notes from the C Major Scale. In this model, the key and the scale match. Presto! We have concordance.

The most effective method to work out the key of a tune

The most straightforward method for working this out is to check out the first and last harmony of the tune. (They're frequently a similar harmony.) close to 100% of the time the key of the melody will be one of those two harmonies.

A key-tracking down model

So for instance, suppose the principal harmony of the tune is A minor.

This implies that you can play any note from the A Minor Scale (or the A Minor Pentatonic Scale) and it will sound great. A few notes will sound better compared to other people, yet not a solitary one of them will sound 'awful'.

How about we check out another model

Suppose the main harmony of the tune was E major. You could play any note from the E Major Scale (or the E Major Pentatonic Scale) and it would sound great.

Contingent upon the track, you may likewise have the option to play the E Minor Scale, or the E Minor Pentatonic Scale as well. Assuming it's a stone track, the E Blues Scale may likewise work.

NINJA TIP: You can frequently play a minor scope over a significant key. This will regularly sound great. This doesn't function too the reverse way around! Attempt it and you'll HEAR the distinction.

CHAPTER 6

STEP BY STEP INSTRUCTIONS TO REHEARSE SCALES

At the point when we learn guitar scales the primary thing we really want to do is submit the scale example to memory.

- The most straightforward method for doing this is to break the scale into reduced down pieces. So as a matter of first importance, center just around box 1 for the scale.

- The notes of all cases cover two octaves. So we can make things much simpler simply by focussing on the primary octave of box 1.

So the least demanding method for learning guitar scales is to 'parted' the scale encloses to octaves 1 and 2.

An illustration of how to become familiar with a guitar scale

We should utilize the G Major Scale for instance. Box 1 resembles this:

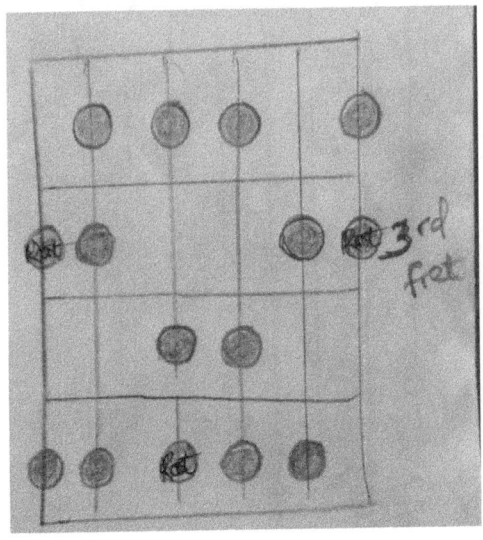

In any case, center around learning the principal octave. This is the separation from the first to the subsequent root note. In this case, for this scale, the main octave traverses strings 6, 5 and 4:

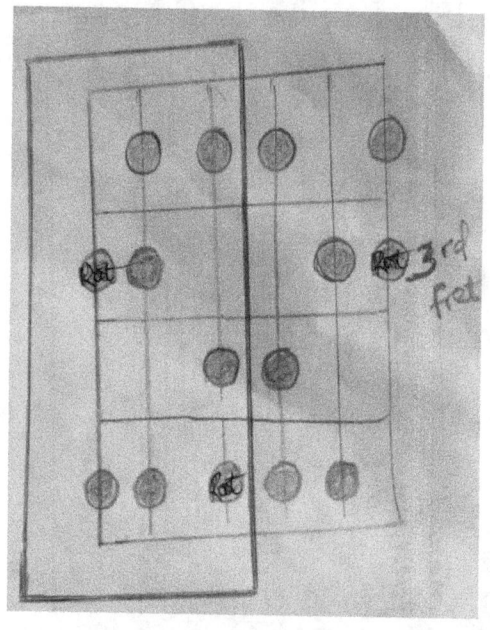

After you've remembered this,
move onto the subsequent octave,
which traverses strings 4 to 1:

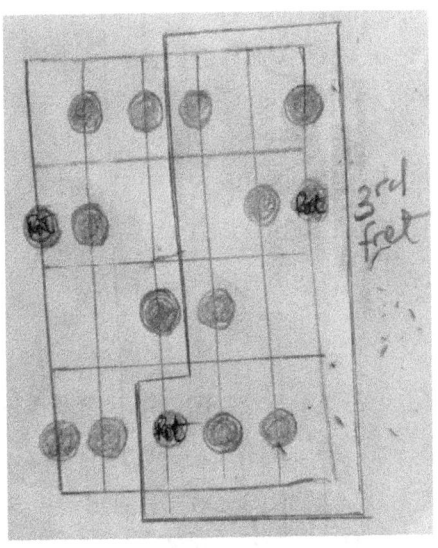

Significant point: Note that the last note of octave 1 is likewise the principal note of octave 2. There are 8 notes in every octave, except there are not 16 notes altogether across two octaves. There are just 15.

Why realize along these lines?

To learn guitar scales we need to break things into reduced down lumps. It simply makes things quicker.

This octave-parting technique probably won't appear to be vital for box 1 of simple examples like the Minor Pentatonic Scale, however for more confounded scales/boxes with more intricate examples this approach can make things much more reasonable and permit us to learn guitar scales rapidly and all the more dependably.

.

Here is a significant piece of procedure

Don't forget to always use one finger for every fret

It's alright to utilize the cushions (the fingerprints) to play notes when you play lead guitar.

This is the kind of thing that ought to be kept away from no matter what while playing harmonies, however while we're attempting to learn guitar scales it's alright to adjust our worrying method. Indeed, it's completely useful! ▯

Advance gradually and accurately to insert great muscle memory

At the point when we learn guitar scales it's vital to advance gradually AND accurately. You should fight the temptation to play quick. Playing gradually and accurately is the most ideal way to implant muscle memory. Playing rapidly prompts missteps, disappointment and jittery muscle memory. That is not what we need.

Work on rising and plummeting the scales, yet in addition have a go at turning around on yourself in various sums.

- For instance: climb two notes, then, at that point, slip one, rise two, then, at that point, plunge one, (etc).

- Then, at that point, have a go at rising 3 and slipping one.

These are valuable ways of learning the scales repetition, obviously we should not fail to focus on the last point here which is to foster a feeling of musicality.

Nothing will work on your capacity to learn guitar scales and play lead guitar more than sticking.

It is fundamental that you play the scales over MUSIC.

Try not to turn into the exemplary room guitarist. The sort of individuals who just learn guitar scales and examples in disconnection. No!

You want to foster a vibe for these examples. Play the scales over sponsorship tracks (YouTube is loaded up with them) and connect and interface with different performers who live locally to you.

Playing with different artists is groundbreaking for your advancement as a guitarist.

Jam exercise - Try this support track

Hit play on the support track beneath and play jam for certain notes from the E Minor Pentatonic Scale:

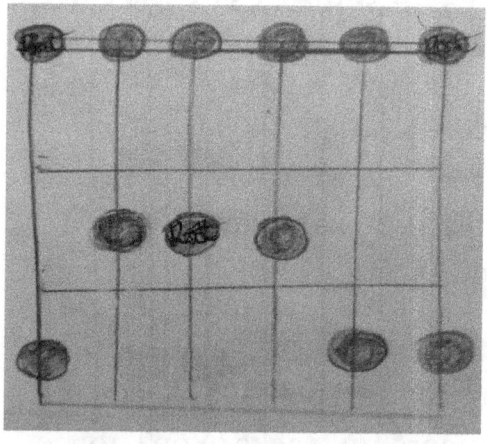

www.ingramcontent.com/pod-product-compliance
Lightning Source LLC
Chambersburg PA
CBHW070139230526
45472CB00004B/1602